Praise for
Healing With Haiku

"*Healing With Haiku* contains Anne's fiery passion for writing and guides readers to insights that pierce through to healing. It is a powerful resource."

—Gary Weinstein, LCSW, therapist

"Anne Helfer has created a delightful guide to healing. Both informative and engaging, Anne presents a clear process to develop the reader's authenticity by writing. In so doing, the reader is engaged in the curiously revealing art of the haiku. What once may have been unclear, this book reveals—both the power of haiku and the authentic self."

—Bill Cross PhD, LMFT, psychotherapist

"*Healing With Haiku* is a phenomenal tool in a therapist's toolbox. The instructions to create and use haiku to access and process emotions are clear and concise, and provides a perfect method for anyone wanting to deepen their knowledge of themselves and transform their emotional landscape. As a clinical psychologist, I will purchase and use this book in my professional practice with patients, and to deepen my own self-understanding."

—Lisa Harrell, PhD, LCP

"Anne helps you to journey through the writing process and form magical haikus that, in turn, help you heal your soul."

—Crystal Pacheco

T0343633

"This workbook is a guide for bringing out the honest truth within, rather than avoiding what needs to be looked at in order to heal. I learned a lot about the structure and ease of writing haiku in this book and highly recommend this technique to anyone seeking fun, creative expression and personal outlet for growth."

—Molly Bondellio, Transformational Yogi and Consciousness Guide and founder of Bhakti Yin Yogi

"What a joy it was, reading and pondering *Healing With Haiku*. The processes are a journey into healing as well as creativity and appreciation for haiku. It's extremely well-written, simple yet deep, and unlike anything I've previously explored. I found the book an excellent tool for healing, growth, and expansion as well as a satisfying read."

—Mary Ellen Popyk, owner of Sanctuary Productions and Spirit Fest Holistic Health Expos

"Through haiku, Anne encourages the reader to delve into the soul, but does so gently, opening the self to deeper understanding. I highly recommend this book for anyone seeking self-exploration and healing."

—Kate Lewis, PhD

"This is a beautiful and artistic work. Powerful and practical, you'll have the benefits of months of insightful therapy for a fraction of the price of one typical therapy session."

—Patrick Ryan

"Superbly crafted, encouraging and accessible, Healing With Haiku should appeal to a broad audience."

—Jikyo Bonnie Shoultz, Sensei, Zen Center of Syracuse

healing
with
haiku

healing with haiku

A POETIC EXPLORATION OF SELF

anne helfer, LCSW

》 hatherleigh

Hatherleigh Press is committed to preserving and protecting the natural resources of the earth. Environmentally responsible and sustainable practices are embraced within the company's mission statement.

Visit us at www.hatherleighpress.com.

Healing With Haiku

Library of Congress Cataloging-in-Publication Data is available.
ISBN: 978-1-961293-14-4

Printed in the United States
10 9 8 7 6 5 4 3 2 1

Contents

Introduction: What Do We Mean by Healing?

> "There is no light without shadow and no
> psychic wholeness without imperfection."
>
> —CARL JUNG

HEALING REFERS TO the process of becoming whole again, and is typically thought of in terms of healing the body after physical injury. In this workbook, however, we will focus on emotional healing, not physical. As a psychotherapist who utilizes creative expression to help clients pay attention to their thoughts and get in touch with their feelings, I know that developing the capacity to explore our inner Selves is crucial to our wellbeing.

Writing is one of the ways we can practice addressing and processing our previously unacknowledged inner truths. The more honest we are with ourselves and the more capable we become in perceiving and accepting the emotions we might tend to avoid—and rediscovering things we have forgotten or repressed—the more complete or whole we can become.

luminous darkness

    glimpsing our shadows can spark

        awareness of truths

the seed was perfect

    fertilize here and prune there

        to bloom in glory

diamond in the rough

    cut then polish to brilliance

        potential revealed

the veil of untruth

    obscuring the light within

        abracadabra!

Why Write?

Many of us believe, "I can't write!" or lament, "I'm a bad speller," or proclaim, "I hated English class in high school!" "I would never choose to use writing as a tool of creativity and personal exploration," they think. To these limiting beliefs, I counter: "Process, not product." Therapeutic writing is *not* about the finished result—the letter, the poem, the journal entry, the article. Writing to heal is about *what* you say, *why* you feel compelled to express it, and *how* you feel while and after you write it.

Although you may never read your words aloud or permit someone else to read them, it is possible that deciding to share these thoughts and feelings with others will bring you deeper healing. Just like a song that touches you deeply, another person might empathize with what you feel and say, creating a bond of understanding and support. However, I wholeheartedly believe that the most important connection you can build is with *yourself*. You need not share your "stuff" with anyone else to benefit from the process of creative self-expression.

writing is healing

   my feelings have to come out

      or I might implode

Numerous studies have shown that writing is beneficial to our mental health. Developing and honing the ability to put our

thoughts down on paper—or on a screen—helps us to know
our Selves better—the sad and the happy, the painful and the
joyous, the calm and the frantic, the guts and the glory.

the hard, sad and cold

reflect soft comfort and warmth

real life is like this

Some folks use journaling to pour out their feelings, to process
stress and discomfort, to explore their inner worlds. Others find
that penning an unedited letter, using it to examine mixed feel-
ings that keep us feeling "stuck," may provide relief from strong
negative emotions. In my therapy practice, it is common that a
client who is struggling in a relationship benefits greatly from
writing a letter to the person they are challenged by, whether a
partner, a parent, a friend or an employer.

I always suggest that they first write an honest, unabridged,
get-it-all-out version—the *unedited* letter—then rewrite it in a
clear, respectful but still truthful manner. Do they have to share
this letter with the intended recipient to find relief? Absolutely
not. Writing therapeutically is primarily about how the process
benefits *the writer* emotionally. Of course, if you think that
sharing your perspective and your truths will positively impact
the relationship, then by all means, send it!

Writing can help us clarify things which seem obscure or out
of reach. How many of us ruminate or spiral, or "can't get out
of our heads?" Written words can help us externalize (perhaps

even *exorcize*) the thoughts that we keep inside, even difficult, deep, hidden, secret feelings—things that, once they find the light of day, help us to better understand our true feelings: grief, fear, anger, jealousy, bitterness, resentment, guilt and shame, yearning, and desire. Writing can dissipate the intensity of our repressed feelings and help us begin to unknot the emotional ball of yarn that can be our minds and hearts, one string, one thought, one emotion at a time.

searing clarity

while painful at times the truth

can illuminate

I wrote the following haiku for a friend who is struggling with alcohol and admitted that he often drinks to avoid feelings of despair. I have suggested that he might put off pouring that glass of wine for a little while and first pay attention to the thoughts and emotions that he is experiencing *before having the drink*. Why? It is possible to diminish the power of our inner world's grip (in his case deep, prolonged sadness) on our subsequent behaviors (excessive alcohol consumption) by releasing the intensity of the emotions through noticing, accepting and tolerating the discomfort.

"sit with that s***" so

the truth of your feelings can

fertilize your growth

Why Haiku?

My first job as a social worker was at an agency where my position was Psychiatric Rehabilitation Counselor, helping people who were diagnosed with severe and persistent mental illnesses. I was tasked with leading groups as well as meeting individually with certain clients for therapy.

Many folks with mental health challenges have personal histories where a positive self-image and strong self-esteem—their *wholeness*—was thwarted early in life, either by growing up in families where abuse and neglect were common or due to the impact of discrimination, poverty, sub-standard schooling or other traumas such as sexual abuse or bullying. Many of these people had also developed addictions, and the combination of ongoing emotional problems plus a lack of healthy social support caused many of these individuals to not function well. Most couldn't get and keep a job, or find appropriate long-term housing, or make and maintain mutually healthy intimate relationships or friendships. Many never finished high school. They often blamed themselves for their situations, though I knew that "environmental failures"—circumstances that are beyond the control of children—were in great part responsible for their development.

grown in rocky soil

   Self arose through the shadows

   guided by the sun

Self forged in the fire

   the crucible sears and brands,

   purifies, transforms

I really wanted to help my clients find and use their voices! Many were "silenced" by their early environments, if they were under-nurtured and under-protected, for example. Consequently, they either never developed, lost touch with, or kept hidden their true Selves while struggling to survive less-than-optimal childhoods and teen years.

silenced by the fear

   of not being heard with love

   find your voice and sing!

shame can silence you

   while the unshackled guilty

   attach the muzzle

To help my clients get in touch with their inner Selves, I created a class called "Writing to Heal." Knowing that the idea of writing can be intimidating to some, I tried to include a variety of forms of writing (letters, short rhyming poems, stream-of-consciousness, letters-to-the-editor, and haikus, for example) that would be of interest to the class members and that required little effort. I emphasized that spelling didn't matter, clarity of handwriting was of no importance, and the breadth of their vocabulary was not a factor in the ability to peer into themselves in order to materialize their thoughts. And, most importantly, they *did not* have to share what they wrote, unless they chose to. After utilizing the curriculum for the very first time, I found that writing haiku seemed to be the easiest and most effective form of written self-expression for the participants. Why?

Answer: haiku is *short*—three lines of verse comprised of seventeen syllables. (Syllabication will be addressed in the following section.)

> **listen to your Self**
>
> **silence the inner critic**
>
> **let your freak flag fly**

Haiku is *easy*—no rhyming necessary!

> **I am a haiku**
>
> **seventeen syllables and**
>
> **three lines of wisdom**

Haiku can speak of serious, esoteric concepts, like the loneliness and existential dread experienced by one of my best friends as he ages without a life partner...

Sisyphean climb

    rough terrain and foggy peak

        desolate plateau

...or be simple and sweet, like this haiku composed by one of my former clients as we were writing about feeling safe and calm.

I love my kitty

    she sits on my lap and purrs

        she is real furry

Traditional haiku is a classic form of poetry known for its brevity, concise use of language, and focus on existential matters, which often contain references to nature. In this workbook, we will learn to write haiku with the goal of exploring our Selves more deeply. Expanding our capacity to notice, explore, and express our emotions is the key to living a more balanced, peaceful and joyous life. Self-knowledge is a hard-earned gift— let's untie the bow!

Classic haiku aims to incorporate certain elements: nature, sensory awareness, self-discovery, a glimpse of enlightenment (the "a-ha moment"), a truth. At the same time, it must adhere to the 5-7-5 syllabic structure: three lines, seventeen syllables. The following poem includes three references to the senses: taste, temperature/touch, and sound. A very simple and common activity—making a cup of tea—comes alive and acquires poetic energy when we pay attention in this way:

(5) mind-ful-ly stir-ring

(7) sweet hon-ey in-to hot tea

(5) the spoon clang deep-ens

—*sweet* [taste]; *hot* [temperature]; *clang* [sound]

Sometimes haiku presents a paradox, a pairing of opposing concepts which at first glance might seem strange yet results in an interesting—even enlightening—truth. I once stopped at a local waterway in the summer to cool off, and decided to sit atop a small boulder in the middle of the creek to meditate. This is the haiku that resulted from that experience:

sitting on a rock

the creek moves relentlessly

grounded in the flow

I was moved in that moment to express that, although life goes on around us and never stops changing, it is possible to experience peace and calm by pausing to observe the impermanence of activity. Change is constant, and the acceptance of that truth can liberate us to live in the moment.

I really love my bed during the long, grey, cold winters we tend to have in central New York State. In order to express the feeling of safety and warmth that I crave during that particular time of year, I use numerous sensory contrasts while also incorporating a reference to the season.

cozy blanket nest

comforts, nurtures and warms me

cold, dark, long winter

Big words or little words. Fancy vocabulary or simple language. Grammar doesn't matter. Proper punctuation? Capitalization? Nope. The only thing that matters is *that you write*.

Structure: Three Lines, Seventeen Syllables

Quick grammar review: a syllable is a unit of pronunciation, the "parts" of a word as we say it aloud. For example, the word "unit" has two syllables, "u-nit," while "pronunciation" has five, "pro-nun-ci-a-tion." As well as the content and meaning and word choice, writing haiku is about the rhythm or the flow of the language as it is read. To be honest though, many of my own creations do not read like music when my focus is on processing emotional content!

There are some words that can be divided up in more than one way. Take the word "family," for example; some folks say "fam-ly" and others say "fam-i-ly"; similarly, "world" can be one syllable or two, "wor-ld." The choices you make while using a word that has more than one acceptable pronunciation demonstrate *poetic license* in action, offering you the freedom to use language as you see fit to effectively express your ideas. I suggest that you write your haikus in pencil with an eraser handy.

As a lover of language, I enjoy moving words around and finding synonyms that have fewer or more syllables than the word that first came to mind. For example, you could use "mad" or "an-gry" or "fur-i-ous" (one, two, three syllables) to express the same idea. Use a thesaurus if you'd like help!

Here is one about a bird's nest that uses "fancy" language:

avian retreat

    that which winter snow reveals

      summer leaves obscure

This haiku instead combines more commonly used words to state the same:

bird nest in a tree

    hidden during summertime

      it cradles snow now

Different words, similar concept. The noun, "bird," is one sylla-
ble and the two-syllable adjective "avian" refers to birds. In the
second haiku, "reveals" implies something that is "hidden" while
"leaves" implies "tree." You have complete freedom to choose
whatever words you want. Both simple, more common words
and fancier, more lofty language are acceptable.

> **Self, core, heart, spirit**
>
> **a rose by any other**
>
> **name is still a rose**

A by-product of writing haiku for emotional expression is
that you might, through this practice, increase your emotional
vocabulary. *Alexithymia* is a concept in the field of psychology
that refers to the inability to know what you are feeling and the
subsequent challenges in talking about your emotions with your
Self or others.

    This can create numerous issues in relationships, because *our
feelings are signals that tell us what our needs are*. It is important
to know what we are feeling, especially when experiencing more
vehement emotions, so we can know what we need *instead* in
order to feel better. Practicing using "feeling words" is helpful
for personal growth as well as relational health.

> **what does my soul need?**
>
> **rain? sun? roots? branching? pruning?**
>
> **constant gardener**

A good friend of mine who experienced emotional neglect as a child and is just now learning to address her long-repressed feelings, wrote the following haiku series, adhering to the 5-7-5 syllabication structure. Notice how many different emotions she expresses!

I feel like a mess

    I can never do things right

        but maybe in time

— *frustration, confusion, hope*

why don't I feel love

    I don't think anyone cares

        can someone love me?

— *loneliness, despondence*

I now feel hopeful

    I can get so sad sometimes

        writing it down helps

— *hope vs. despair*

surrounded by walls

    these four walls don't talk to me

        outside is scary

—*fear, loneliness, paranoia*

don't ever say bye

    because if you say goodbye

        all I'll do is cry

—*fear of abandonment, loss, loneliness*

he doesn't show love

    my dad doesn't love enough

        wish I saw him more

—*sadness, disconnection, confusion*

Finally, she decides that self-respect trumps self-neglect:

I don't think I want

    to be around anyone

        who doesn't love me

—*clarity, self-concern, growth*

My goal with this book is not to make you write precisely crafted and poetically profound haikus. My purpose is solely to assist you in learning how to write one of the most simple and concise forms of poetry in order to discover and express what is *true to you*—and hopefully to enjoy doing so!

You can keep it simple, or you can dig deep. You can write about pleasant or satisfying moments, called *glimmers*, or uncomfortable or painful ideas and feelings. Emphasizing the happy can keep you focused on noticing the good things in your life—like a butterfly on a flower or a fulfilling marriage—and help you feel gratitude. Attention to the challenging parts of your life can help lessen the emotional load you may be carrying as you "let go" of the tough stuff.

while triggers portend

deep darkness and pain, glimmers

signal hope and light

Haiku is concise, condensed: nature, emotion, and simplicity merge together to create profound insights within just seventeen syllables. With your new understanding of its basic structure and themes, the groundwork is laid for crafting your own verses, and thus beginning your own healing process by exploring new perspectives. As we turn the page to the next chapter, prepare to unleash your creativity as I guide you in writing your own unique haiku, breathing life into your thoughts and surroundings through poetry.

Let's Write!

LET'S START SIMPLY with haikus about nature. These serve two purposes: First, as stated in the previous chapter, traditional haiku often contains a reference to nature—the weather, a season, animals, plants, or the elements of fire, wind, sky, water, or earth. Secondly, many people find pleasure, peace or healing while outdoors, whether in the woods, at the beach, hiking a mountain, visiting a park, gardening, birdwatching or camping. Remember: our overarching goal is to guide you toward emotional healing, exploring both *the good* to lift your spirits and *the bad* to release a burden.

what are raspberries

but red rubies on the bush

nature's juicy gems

Keeping to the 5-7-5 structure—editing as you go if necessary, moving words around or using synonyms—choose a pleasant topic and write! Please note: If you are inspired to write more than there is space for here, you can use the blank pages at the end of the workbook for these bonus creations.

Prompts on Nature

If you are stuck, here are some suggestions: your favorite season, a wild animal you'd like to be, a childhood memory that occurred outdoors, a beautiful travel destination.

5

7

5

Now for something specific. Try writing a haiku about springtime. I'll start:

phlox greets me in June

first with sweet spring aroma

then soothing color

5

7

5

What does winter feel like for you? Have you lived in various places where wintertime expresses herself differently? Maybe you have never experienced a "real" winter, but you would like to. Try to express these feelings in your word choice.

5

7

5

Recall a spectacular outdoor location you've visited. Describe it, using language that evokes the feelings of being in that place.

5

7

5

Write a haiku about the weather. Sounds simple, right? Focus on weather conditions you most enjoy, or most dislike—whatever inspires the clearest feelings in you.

dazzle the diamonds

    sunny frigid winter morn

        brilliant glitter snow

5

7

5

Let's try something more concrete and smaller in scale. Consider a flower, plant, bush or tree. Write a haiku about the feelings it inspires.

5

7

5

Staying on theme, let's have a haiku here about an animal or an insect.

5

7

5

Write about the majesty or awe you can find in nature. I'll give you an example first:

the rainbow paints hope

transforming teardrops into

colorful brilliance

5

7

5

Of course, sometimes nature can be hostile, dangerous. Think of an unrelenting blizzard, a devastating flood, desert-like heat and dryness, a voracious lion, an angry dog prone to biting, beestings, hurricanes, avalanches. Now, create a haiku of your own that expresses how nature can be as destructive as it is beautiful.

my oppressors, like

quicksand, immobilize me

yet my spirit soars

5

7

5

Just as the experience of ambivalence or mixed emotions may confuse us, nature can straddle the line between being beneficial or noxious; she can be both life-affirming and life-threatening. Consider:

the very same rain

that quenches thirsty seedlings

drowns treed mountainsides

You could try to capture the sun or the wind here in a similar vein, or a beautiful yet poisonous plant, or the pros and cons of a partic-ular season.

woodland creatures know

which juicy red berries are

delight or demise

5

7

5

For this final haiku, choose your own topic from the natural world. What does nature mean to you? How can you bring those feelings into your Self? How can you express it?

5

7

5

As you can see, composing haiku about nature is much more involved than writing about a sunny sky or a rainy day. The sheer variety of topics that present when observing nature lends itself to countless interpretations. As we close this chapter on capturing the beauty and the brawn of nature through haiku, it's time to shift our focus from the intricate details of the natural world to the light and shadow of human emotions. Just as each season stirs feelings within us, so too can our experiences of joy, love, and tranquility inspire new avenues of poetic expression. To begin, we'll explore the "sunshine" of the human soul—the positive emotions that make up what we call happiness.

Positive Emotions

Love

WHAT *is* LOVE, anyway? *Love* means different things to different people: loyalty, caring, desire, selflessness, trust, emotional warmth. Love for your child feels distinct from love for a partner. Love for your country is not the same as a love of music. Is love passion? Affection? Devotion? Companionship? Safety? Comfort? Compassion? I'm not certain what love is, but I know the many ways it can feel.

> **touch is medicine**
>> **for my body, elixir**
>>> **for my lonesome soul**

comfort and pleasure

    your body is my shelter

        soothing, strong heartbeat

love is the anchor

    making safe harbor where our

        souls can freely float

spirit rising through

    resurrected libido

        your touch is divine

I want a man who

    gazes with adoration

        at me like my dog

Anyhow, it doesn't matter what *I* think or feel; what matters here is what *you* experience when writing about love. Let's haiku!

Prompts on Love

Let's start with an "easy" one. Odds are, you have some feelings about the idea of romantic love. Express this in haiku.

5

7

5

Physical passion: often a component of romantic love, and one which people have been composing poems about (in all manner of forms) for centuries. Why don't you try your hand at it?

like moth to the flame

my heart craves you and fears you

incinerate me

5

7

5

How about friendship? The bond between friends is a special kind of love, one well worth exploring in haiku. For me, friendship is a source of warmth and energy in my life. How does friendship feel to you?

connecting with you

rekindled my spark for life

thank you from the heart

5

7

5

Unique from friendship, the love we bear for a sibling, a parent, child, or any family member can be a source of comfort and strength in even the most difficult of times. What does family mean to you?

5

7

5

Here's one: have you ever experienced spiritual love? This could be a sense of love emanating from the Divine, or a feeling of connection with another person that goes beyond any kind of physical attraction, a true communion between souls. It's a big idea to squeeze into just 17 syllables…but let's give it a try together!

fierce and luminous

    your heart is a sun, burning

        with the truth of love

5

7

5

While we do want to focus on its many positives, there is no denying that love can be a source of great pain in our lives: whether from unrequited love, a death, abandonment, or a break-up. Together, let's try to contain the feeling of love's pain in haiku, that we might better understand it.

mopping up the tears
emotional janitors
repair broken hearts

5

7

5

Here's a question: does the experience of receiving love and feeling loved yourself differ from offering love to another? Can you express what it's like for you to feel loved?

5

7

5

Now, let's write about something you "love" in the more casual sense of the word. What food makes you drool? Is there a musical style you prefer? Have you ever had a celebrity crush? Do you really, really like a particular song, film, or book? Why do you "love" this? How does this "love" make you feel inside?

5

7

5

Prompts on Trust

I include trust here as a close cousin to love. Of course, we can trust people whom we don't necessarily love—you might confidently trust your dentist to fix your broken tooth, for example. We can also love people but not trust them, such as a family member who often shares information that you tell them in confidence. Synonyms for *trust* might include *confidence, dependence, reliance.*

Who can you trust, and with what? How do you express what it feels like to you to trust someone?

---

trust lets others in

connected and protected

embodied feeling

5

7

5

Have you ever trusted someone you were very close to, then lost that trust? What happened? How does losing trust impact the feelings you have toward another person? Perhaps you feel confused, betrayed, lost. When the ability to confide in, depend upon or rely on someone disappears, what happens inside your mind and body and heart?

self-sufficiency

 flooded my bones and my brain

  when trust was poisoned

I will not trust an

 Other with my Self ever

  who else can know Me?

5

7

5

I think "belonging" fits into the category of love, when broadly defined, and certainly goes hand in hand with relationships of trust. When we are comfortable in a group or a community because we have common interests or share similar values, we belong. We feel seen and heard while enjoying being a part of something larger than ourselves; when we experience this connectivity, we might feel love, or loved. Where do you belong?

5

7

5

Or perhaps you feel a desire to belong, but haven't yet found your community. Perhaps you are a maverick who does not care to fit in, or a lone wolf who sometimes desires company? Haiku here about your personal experience with belonging!

5

7

5

Pleasure

Can you recall the lightness of spirit you may have felt as a child? Did you chase bubbles or bat a balloon around, just because? Hang on the monkey bars or climb a tree? Dance with abandon? Did you act silly for no particular reason except for feeling lighthearted and spontaneous and free? Do you still giggle?

go out of your mind

and get into your body

it's a no-brainer

I contend that when we are moved to do things "for no reason," we are not in our heads and minds but instead in our bodies and our emotions. We are *feeling*, not *thinking*. So now, let's permit our brains take a break and recharge our Selves by expressing mindless, uncalculated, spontaneous, simple pleasures.

two squirrels chasing

    each other…playing? mating?

        must be teenagers

autumn leaves adorn

    lady trees with brilliant gems

        rubies and topaz

cheerful spring birds sing

    and fly and eat, play and mate

        ignorance is bliss

The next haiku, inspired during a walk on a winter afternoon, reflects my adult perspective toward what I once enjoyed doing as a child. That day, I did in fact stick out my tongue and chase a few flakes, yet my pleasure was tainted by the thought of ecological devolution.

catching snowflakes on

my tongue…lighthearted pleasure

or poisonous ice?

Prompts on Pleasure

What makes you feel light? What was the last silly or goofy thing you did? Have you done anything spontaneous lately? Have you giggled out loud?

---

cha cha cha tango

my id dances with ego

superego bows

5

7

5

Contentment is a sense of satisfaction in the present moment, feeling okay with the way things are right now. It is peaceful to have no worries about the past and no concern for the future. Write about this experience now.

life can be simple

    eat, sleep, move, love, give and take

        back to the garden

early morning peace

    dog cat birds breeze…backyard joy

        heaven here on earth

envious of clouds

    who, just doing what they do,

        float without desire

5

7

5

What makes you happy? What puts a big smile on your face and lightens your step, expands your chest, lifts your spirits? (Notice that a feeling of happiness is often expressed through a sense of becoming lighter and more expansive.)

> my happy place is
>> when body, mind and spirit
>>> dance at the same time

5

7

5

Which do you prefer: contentment or happiness? Are they the same?
Do they feel different in your mind? In your body?

5

7

5

Now write about joy. What makes your heart sing or your cheeks hurt from smiling? Have you ever cried with joy, with tears welling up in your eyes or streaming down your cheeks? Do you experience joy only in your mind, as a thought or an idea, or do you feel it in your body as well?

5

7

5

How about ecstasy? We understand ecstasy to be truly overwhelming joy, a feeling of happiness and fulfilment so overpowering that we cannot speak, can barely think. How would you capture in haiku the feeling of being so happy that words fail you?

5

7

5

Now for you to put your own spin on things. Compose your own haiku about anything that brings you pleasure.

5

7

5

Peacefulness

an ocean of peace

can smooth the rocks in our soul

breathe waves of solace

It can be quite difficult to enjoy a sense of natural calm for many folks nowadays; modern life seems to require us to be "on" much of the time, making even the thought of relaxing for a moment daunting or guilt-laden. Yet science confirms what we know intuitively: it is important to slow down, to take breaks, and to rest. "Peace and quiet" not only benefits our physical health but our relationships with family, friends, and *especially with ourselves.*

My belief is that we have—to humanity's detriment— been hijacked in numerous ways by an overdependence on technology, and it seems that humans, particularly at work, are expected to function more and more like machines. There is even a term in Japanese, *karoshi,* that means "death by overwork."

work to live or live

    to work? "productivity"

    can work us to death

Our ability to maintain physical energy, mental clarity and emotional balance depends on how well we eat, how much we move our bodies, and the quality of our sleep. Nowadays, too many of us struggle simply to get a good night's sleep. I believe that we have lost a healthy respect for the role of rest and the necessary process of *gearing down* in order to permit sleep to naturally overcome us. When the demands of modern life to "keep doing more, faster" overwhelm our organism's capacity to adapt, we can experience burnout.

too much on my plate

    my life is a banquet and

    I'm already stuffed

I am a human!

not a machine! and I must

eat, sleep, move, breathe, love

Would you prefer to relax and de-stress on a regular basis to avoid becoming overwhelmed, or do you tend to push yourself to the brink (or over it) of physical, emotional and mental exhaustion? Are you a human *being* or a human *doing*?

escaping jet speed

parachute at the ready

slow float on the wind

To practice getting in touch with the ways you might prefer to feel to instead of being "tired but wired," let's now focus on some emotional states that are antidotes to stress by exploring what makes us feel comforted and relaxed. Paying attention to pleasant sensory input can calm the nervous system and give our minds a rest. Touch, sounds, and smells are three ways we can tune out our thinking, always-analyzing minds and tune in via the body to the present moment.

Prompts on Peacefulness

Touch. *Is there a person, a pet, or an object that brings a sense of peace or comfort to you through touch? A summer breeze on a hot day? A stuffed animal or blankie you loved as a child? A hug or caress from your partner? A favorite sweater? What sorts of things do you like to touch to put your Self at ease?*

---

    hammock love, rock me

       baby like a woman, warm

          cozy safe cocoon

5

7

5

Hearing. *Are there sounds that induce a sense of relaxation when you hear them? The crackling of a campfire? Ocean surf? The breeze in the trees? Your grandpa's voice on the phone? Of course, sounds can also energize us, such as a song or piece of music that invigorates you; you can write about that instead if you choose. Maybe silence is peaceful for you.*

birdsong greets the morn

after noon, cicadas buzz

crickets welcome dusk

5

7

5

Smell. *Some say that smell is one of our most powerful senses. Just one whiff of a particular scent can transport us to the past or remind us of a person we have a positive connection with. Smells might bring up memories of events or places we have enjoyed. I'm reminded now of the many smells that the New York State Fair offers, a place with many happy associations from my childhood. Some of us may experience nostalgia through the scent of the ocean or the aromas of a backyard barbecue.*

wet worms, rainy days

    wood smoke and plum tree blossoms

        perfuming my world

5

7

5

Is there a particular smell that evokes a sense of calm, comfort or peace for you? A pot of soup on the stove? A certain scent found in nature? Another person's scent?

5

7

5

What else might provide you with a sense of peace? A place, ritual, or certain people? Can you describe what peacefulness feels like in your body?

5

7

5

Some folks feel centered and calm when they are "in the flow" of exercising, dancing, singing, creating art, playing an instrument or during sex. For me, meditation calms both body and mind. How do you experience peace and calm? Perhaps in your chest or belly? Does your breathing slow and do your muscles relax? Or do you experience peace only in your mind?

movement and stillness

  breathe in and out to quiet

  both body and mind

dark, safe peacefulness

  sleep is the next best thing to

  a quiet womb float

5

7

5

Emotionally speaking, feeling peaceful typically involves a lack of distress and an absence of internal conflict or agitation which allows us to feel calm and comfortable. For many of us, this feeling can arise from a sense of belonging, when we are with trusted people who care about us and "have our backs." This type of peace may feel like an open-heartedness or an expansive and light energy in our chests or an empty, spacious or floaty mind. Do you ever feel open-hearted, safe and relaxed in the presence of others? Write about that now.

strong arms, stronger heart

my head rests on your warm chest

I feel so safe now

sense of belonging

and internalized safety

spacious heart, calm gut

your pain is my pain

    open hearts collect tears like

        a curved leaf holds dew

5

7

5

Many people aren't as eager for company or companionship, as they might find other people annoying, boring, or anxiety-provoking. Some folks just prefer to be alone occasionally, frequently, or always. If you are only able to access tranquility when alone, write about that experience. Perhaps you could write about the difference between loneliness and solitude.

      tranquility purrs

         when I am alone but then

            I can feel lonely

5

7

5

Prompts on Equanimity

Equanimity *describes a state in which—particularly when facing a stressor—you experience an evenness of mind and a lack of emotional reactivity. It refers to an ultimate sense of balance. Despite what is happening around or inside of you, equanimity is the capacity to maintain your composure through a deep acceptance of what is. Equanimity is tranquility, mental steadiness and emotional stability in the face of external or internal distress.*

---

surfing hurricanes

the buoyant soul can also

on calm water float

clouds hover, wind whips

lightning strikes, hail pelts…will you

take cover or stand?

5

7

5

This next haiku was inspired by my introduction to snorkeling in the ocean, which happened to occur on a blustery day. I realized that, although the waves were a foot high, I needed to ride the surface and float with the movement rather than try to push through or fight the waves. Have you ever experienced a similar moment of clarity, a feeling of oneness and serenity within your surroundings?

in choppy waters

surrender, not effort, leads

to peaceful floating

5

7

5

Now write about a time that you may have felt serene even while
under pressure; can you remember how you maintained your calm?
(By the way, "e-qua-ni-mi-ty" is a five-syllable word!)

calm despite chaos

 deeply rooted in the flow

  heart of hurricane

real sends me reeling

 open and present to pain

  wobble but don't fall

5

7

5

Prompts on Relief

Feeling *relief* occurs when distress or suffering has diminished or ceased. I think the word relief implies a sense of peace, whether it's the relaxation felt after having completed a challenging task (an "aah" moment) or lifted weight mingled with sorrow when a loved one who has been living with chronic and debilitating pain finally passes away.

Sometimes we experience relief—a letting go—when we share a painful secret with a trusted ally. Anything that makes you think or feel or say "Whew! I'm glad that's over" signals the calm of relief.

---

exhale fear and hate

heart and soul balanced through breath

inhale peace and love

feelings come and go

the future becomes the past

and this too shall pass

5

7

5

Let's get physical. How does it feel to have a cool drink on a swel-
tering day? A hot bath when chilly? A massage when tense? Eating
good food when your tummy is growling and you are light-headed
with hunger? Try writing about this sort of relief, the calm that
surfaces when we directly counter or remove sensory discomfort.

roast? nah! drown? un huh!

when hell or high water comes

I hope to float cool

5

7

5

Capturing our happiest moments in haiku—while simultane-
ously identifying the pleasure we may be missing—lets us reflect
with greater clarity on all the best parts of our life. It helps us
appreciate what we have now while identifying what we want to
obtain in the future. This type of focus is made possible through
the deceptively simple form of seventeen syllables, purpose-
fully arranged. In celebrating the beauty of positive emotions
through haikus, we've practiced expressing joy, gratitude, and
love by casting light on the everyday moments that uplift us.

However, just as the sun casts shadows, so too do our hearts, minds and bodies hold space for the complexities of negative emotions. If you're seeking healing through haiku, you're likely familiar with the impact our darker feelings can have on the course of one's life. In the next section of this workbook, we will explore how these darker feelings can also be harnessed into haikus, transforming pain, sadness, and anger into poignant expressions of the human experience, allowing us to better navigate our own emotional landscape.

Difficult Feelings

Sadness

Feeling sad usually has to do with the *loss* of something we value. Sadness may result from situations like the death of a loved one; an old friend whom you haven't seen for years backing out of a lunch date; your favorite band's long-anticipated live show getting cancelled. When we value or appreciate something and lose it (or are never able to have it), we naturally feel sad.

> **melancholia**
> > **beautiful word for lonely**
> > > **and lost connections**

missing what is gone

grief is not the enemy

love and loss are friends

is it better to

have never loved or to have

love and then lose it?

Sometimes other people hurt us, causing us emotional pain.
A cruel word aimed at us may cause humiliation and a *loss* of
pride. If a partner is unfaithful, we can *lose* our bond and trust in
them. Betrayal shakes our reality, creating a *loss* of stability and
certainty. When a confidante shares a secret we have entrusted
them with, our perception of safety is altered and we might
consider distancing ourselves from them or abandoning the
relationship altogether, threatening a *loss* of connection and
belonging. Broken promises can cause us to feel neglected or
unimportant, jolting our sense of identity and worthiness, cre-
ating a *loss* of "mattering" to others.

Feeling invalidated—questioning our relevance to oth-
ers—can impact our sense of wholeness, our integrity, and our
self-esteem. When others hurt us, we might feel that our value
has been diminished.

lonely children know

    that there is no place like home

        no soft place to fall

emotional scars

    cracking through memory's scab

        nightmares and flashbacks

Prompts on Sadness

Have you ever lost the trust you had in someone or something (a business, a political party, a community group, for example) because they betrayed you in some fashion? Did you believe in a particular person's or group's values until they stopped meeting your standards, at which point you lost both faith and confidence in their motives or behaviors? Did this betrayal only impact your mind and thinking, or did you feel it in your body as well?

---

they hobbled my heart
    no one protected it from
        loneliness and pain

pull close or push back?
    betrayal is confusing
        connect or protect?

5

7

5

Sadness may feel like an inner emptiness, or it might fill us up with pain. We may each experience sadness differently, sensing it perhaps in the heart or the belly or throughout the body. How does sadness feel to you?

needing in the void

   unbearable disconnect

      turn off your feelings

5

7

5

Some folks manage to avoid having this normal-yet-uncomfortable emotion altogether, bypassing the pain of loss and the embarrassment and helplessness that one might experience when feeling vulnerable. Keep in mind that you may even experience sadness in entirely different ways in response to different events over the course of your life. However, whether you tend to be a holder-inner or a letter-outer, I personally know and professionally attest that "the feeling is the healing."

Can you describe a time when expressing your sadness made you feel better? Or if not, can you imagine what that release might feel like?

---

psychotherapy

　　open-heart surgery with

　　　　empathic scalpel

5

7

5

Who or what has hurt you recently? Nobody goes through life without getting at least a few bumps and bruises, so odds are you have at least one recent grievance.

to get your needs met

you hurt me then you left me

sacrificial lamb

5

7

5

Let's go back a bit. It's the traditional approach of, "Tell me a little bit about your childhood." Can you write about something that made you sad as a child?

tender becomes tense

when gentle hearts beat alone

pain toughens them up

5

7

5

Fast forward to the present. What saddens you now? Where do you feel the hurt in your body?

primal connection

so far from fire and tribe

I miss the circle

5

7

5

Loss is one of the most common causes of sadness. Have you lost a pet, or a friend, or a family member? What do you miss about them?

5

7

5

Grief is a deep sadness, a sense of heart-breaking loss. The word
bereave means to deprive or take away; we grieve that which was
taken from us, depriving us of something we valued or needed.
Have you ever felt grief? Are you grieving now?

having no anchor

   liberating or lonely?

     floating or drowning?

5

7

5

Have you ever felt lonely? Occasionally? Never? All the time? Humans are social creatures, although some of us are less social than others. Write about how or when you experience loneliness, if in fact you do.

chameleon-like, I
   can get in but don't fit in
      searching to belong

I am a rock and
   —archipelagos connect—
      I am an island

5

7

5

Prompts on Jealousy

Jealousy and envy can also stem from sadness. Jealousy is when we're sad—and possibly frustrated—because we want but don't have what someone else has, and envy is when we're saddened by someone else's possessions, success or good fortune.

Jealousy is often a hard thing to admit, and when it is paired with a sense of injustice, it can develop into bitterness. We might feel angry and sad that we don't have something that other people have, *especially* if we were deprived through no fault of our own, or if the other people have what we lack simply due to good fortune, not any personal efforts.

What, or who, are you jealous of?

5

7

5

I sometimes feel envious of people who have (or had) close rela-tionships with their mothers. I know that this jealousy stems from losing my mom at a young age and the pain I still feel about not having maternal love, care, and concern now and when I became a mother myself. This sadness reflects a void that was never filled, which surfaces as "jealousy" when I see others being "mothered," even as adults.

our childhood needs of

nurture, protection, comfort

are never outgrown

5

7

5

Do you feel jealousy about something you never had in your life that others have easy access to?

the hungry heart craves

internal security

desperate to bond

5

7

5

Life is unfair, and sometimes it is daunting to accept this unjust truth. Have you ever felt bitterness because of this? What caused those thoughts? How did they feel? Were they fleeting or did they linger?

if she had died I'd

    understand her disconnect

        but mom's still alive

is it just to take

    from undeserving wealthy

        to balance the scales?

5

7

5

Repressing Emotions

When emotions are repressed or suppressed rather than experienced or expressed, we might become depressed. This belief was the impetus for creating this workbook, and my work as a therapist centers on helping people acknowledge, experience and process emotions in a healthy way, *particularly* the ones that we prefer to avoid. *Healing With Haiku* is a part of this process.

When we make it a habit to externalize what we tend to hold in, we no longer internalize the emotional energy that can wreak havoc with our inner peace. To quote Cat Stevens (now known as Yusuf Islam) in his song "Father and Son": "All the times I've cried, keeping all the things I knew inside, *it's hard, but it's harder to ignore it.*" Only once we believe it's okay, even necessary, to know and perhaps share all of our truth, then we can begin to heal.

fear and loss are friends

    my strength is in my weakness

        I know high and low

sacred space for Self

    the truth is hard and easy

        confessional booth

Sometimes *internal* pressure—coming from the Self—causes us to hold things in. We might have thoughts like "I don't want to be a burden," "No one will understand," "I shouldn't be so upset," "I should be able to handle this myself." Even if we don't say such things aloud, we might believe them subconsciously.

Sometimes *external* pressure from others makes us want to contain our feelings. A history of being ridiculed for crying, for example, or being criticized for being "too sensitive," or being raised to believe that anger is unacceptable can teach us to mask our emotions or even shut down before we ever express them aloud. Many of us grew up in environments where showing and sharing our feelings was uncomfortable or unsafe, so we learned to keep our emotions hidden.

And some folks—to avoid experiencing distress when comfort or release is not possible—default to self-distraction or emotional numbing. But if we permit ourselves to experience and express our thoughts and feelings, we can release this stuck energy and instead begin to sense peace, dignity, and freedom.

Here are some expressions we use to talk about how we contain our feelings:

grin and bear it	repress	paralyze
control yourself	stuff	soldier through
suck it up	numb out	stomach it
feeling stuck	internalize	bite your tongue
hold it in	shut down	clam up
closed up	suppress	black out
swallow your feelings	freeze up	keep a lid on it

Have you ever found yourself using language like this to describe what you feel—or, rather, what you refuse to feel? Did anyone ever tell you to contain your emotions using such words? Did you ever tell yourself something like that? Consider whether such language is really a healthy way to talk about our emotions. Just because this is what we learned, whether from neglect, abuse, bullying, or cultural norms, doesn't mean that we have to continue to believe it.

Write about depression here: yours, a friend's, a family member's.
Remember, don't suppress or repress; rather, EXPRESS yourself!

violent weeding

anger, rejection and pain

yanked out from deep roots

the failure to mourn

when early loss hits portends

a life full of grief

5

7

5

Anger

Anger is a natural, healthy response to injustice and disrespect. How we feel it, process it, and express it is of utmost importance. When fight energy is aroused in us, our hearts may pound, our muscles may tighten, and our digestion slows or stops.

Contraction occurs when we hold anger in. This implosion, or turning in against the Self, contributes to tension, pain, panic, depression, and anxiety. Chronically repressed anger can lead to hypertension, cardiac symptoms, digestive disorders, autoimmune conditions, and self-harming behaviors like cutting or addiction.

Expansion occurs when we act out our anger. We might explode, attacking other people with our words or with our bodies, or even damage property. This forceful, albeit natural, energetic experience can be dangerous, because out-of-control rage might include yelling, screaming, name-calling, hitting, throwing objects, sexual assault, destructive vandalism, and armed conflict resulting in maiming or killing.

> **protect at all costs**
>
> > **do what it takes to survive**
> >
> > > **guns were once fire "arms"**

> **excessive pressure**
>
> > **self-destruct or release it**
> >
> > > **implode or explode**

The ideal expression of anger is to speak up when we sense it—either by responding directly to the person(s) who hurt us or by venting confidentially to a non-involved party. Asserting yourself is not always an easy task, however. If you can't counter the perceived insult or injustice directly and/or immediately, the next best thing is to internally acknowledge your reaction.

Conscious awareness of anger will help to keep the feeling from simmering subconsciously within your being, just waiting to boil over when a similar offense occurs. It is helpful to notice how your body feels with the energy of self-protective arousal.

> **how to lead with light?**
>
> > **be the voice of the oppressed**
> >
> > > **heart afire, words sear**
>
> > **silenced by shame, but**
> >
> > > **the predator bears the blame**
> > >
> > > > **shout aloud their name!**

When something happens that offends our integrity or our sense of fairness, it is natural to want to "right the wrong"; however, *unacknowledged* anger has serious power to hurt us. In my therapy practice, it is common for individuals who are experiencing depression to either subconsciously or actively suppress their frustration, resentment and anger, sometimes chronically. Instead of being aware of their true (even if negative, strong, or "socially unacceptable") feelings, they tend to default to self-blame because, ironically, it is "safer" to feel angry with themselves than it is to confront the actual origin of their discomfort.

Guilt and shame can paralyze us emotionally, inhibiting the drive to actively defend ourselves, resulting in directing our "fight" energy inward. This undischarged energy can disrupt our inner balance, making us feel quite edgy, anxious, or even panicky, resulting in systemic dysregulation. It takes a lot of energy to contain our energy! Our primitive drive is to attack when perceiving a threat, but we are often socially trained to "play nice."

lose your Self to keep

   the peace…or find your true Self

      by keeping your peace

In line with the purpose of this workbook, I want to re-emphasize that there is nothing wrong with the emotion of anger; it is, in fact, beneficial, as it sends us a message that something is not right. As explained above, anger is only problematic when we either suppress it (hurting ourselves) or act on it with aggression (hurting others). In this section, we will practice noticing what actually causes us to experience anger, keeping in mind that its healthy release can lead to calm, comfort, balance, and more peaceful ways of interbeing.

anger motivates

protect and defend...survive

when we care we rage

Anger is a very potent and important emotion, not only in that it can feel quite impressive in the body (rising heat, shakiness, chest tension, clenched fists and jaw, quickening heart, etc.) but this common yet commonly suppressed (and repressed) feeling is, in its essence, protective of the Self. Anger and its stronger cousin, rage, often arise in response to injustice, disrespect, or abuse.

When someone takes something of yours that you value, you might feel irritated or enraged. A friend calls you a pejorative name? "How dare she!" you might think. Either she is wrong and doesn't know you well, or she is right and the truth hurts, or maybe she was deliberately trying to wound you.

Whatever the truth is, a sense of hurt often underlies anger. While being hurt can make us feel vulnerable, anger, in contrast, can feel empowering. While men are typically more comfortable with the experience of anger, numerous female clients of mine have commented that they cry when, in truth, they are angry! In extreme cases, it is possible that we might suffer from *angrophobia*, which is a fear of feeling anger.

avodance of pain

is suffering, acceptance

releases the truth

I can get quite frustrated when I am misunderstood by people whom I value. When someone close to me either doesn't listen well or disregards my concerns, I feel as if they don't care about me. Whenever things that matter to us are under attack, it is normal to feel like an injustice has occurred and then to want to right the wrong or force the person to reconsider. This is the energy of anger, which represents the fight response that we all are born with: You're wrong about me! Don't you care? Why are you doing this? Hey, that hurts! That's mine and I earned it; how dare you take it? Don't do that, my friend!

Prompts on Anger

Let's start low on the Mad-o-Meter. What is something that bugs you? Bothers you? Annoys you? Maybe it's a pesky mosquito or unrelenting rain, cold French fries, or hearing your partner tell the same story you have already heard hundreds of times. What makes your eyes roll up? Hypocrisy and indifference annoy me:

---

caring is active

    not passive: "thoughts and prayers"

        don't walk the true walk

5

7

5

Now let's write about frustration. When tension is building a bit, what causes you to grit your teeth or grunt quietly? What disappoints you? What causes your face to feel warm or makes you think "if this doesn't stop I'm gonna…"

empty tube of glue

always fixing the broken

but solvents persist

5

7

5

Consider all the petty frustrations of everyday life. Is the bus you take to work running late for the third day in a row? Is the neighbor's dog barking yet again? Does your sleep mate keep you awake with their snoring more nights than not? Is a less productive and younger colleague getting promoted while you aren't? In a culture focused on consumption and pressuring us to keep up, it is easy to get frustrated.

FOMO is "fear of

   missing out"; I have FOKU

     "fear of keeping up"

5

7

5

Next, write about something that makes you mad. Do you feel angry when someone disrespects you, or when you get cut off in traffic? As a mother, I'm mad when I have to say, "I've told you a hundred times to....!" Do you act on that feeling, or are you able to control your reaction?

pirates of pleasure

we are burning our own ship

hoarding stuff, not soul

5

7

5

Rage and fury are out of control feelings of anger. Have you ever "lost it?" What happened? Did you contain the energy you felt, or did you release it in some way?

rage flows in my veins

my heart growls deep inside

like a cornered dog

5

7

5

Can you think of something that used to enrage you but doesn't any longer? Is there a person or a situation that used to irritate you to the point of explosion but does not impact you as strongly now? Or still infuriates, but you have learned to let go of its power over you? What might help you to think "and this too shall pass?"

5

7

5

Resentment and its stronger counterpart, bitterness, are anger focused against an element of injustice. Beneath resentment is the sense that things are unfair and that you deserve better. Maybe you believe that you should be treated more respectfully or that you are missing out on something others have and damn it, you think you should have it too. Bitterness is resentment magnified; it feels deeper, harder, harsher, more emotionally painful. As uncomfortable as it may be, try to write about feeling resentful or bitter now.

the neglected one

had to reach out to get help

what an irony

"resilient" my ass!

needing in the void, alone

and scared, do or die

5

7

5

Fear

Fear is defined by Merriam-Webster as "an unpleasant, often strong, emotion caused by anticipation or awareness of danger." Fear is related to numerous emotions: anxiety, fright, dread, panic, terror, and disgust (which signals contamination and the possibility of danger in the form of illness or death). All are connected in some way with feeling unsafe and out of control.

> **holding us hostage**
>> **to the past and future fear**
>>> **is a terrorist**

Just like other emotions, feeling afraid has many degrees: concern, apprehension, nervousness, anxiety, fear, terror. Low-level fear, such as concern or worry, is experienced primarily as mental distress with minimal physiological activation. Apprehension or nervousness are stronger feelings that, if you are paying attention, can be sensed in the body.

Similar to how embarrassment (defined as self-conscious distress, arising when you're *afraid* that someone will judge your behavior) may make us blush, nervousness may appear in the body as hand wringing, toe-tapping, or irregular eye movement. When apprehensive, we may be "on the lookout," extra vigilant, although we might not be able to pinpoint what exactly we are expecting to happen.

Prompts on Fear

Uncertainty is a source of fear for many people. Can you write about something that makes you nervous? A person? A situation?

---

heightened awareness

is it sensitivity?

hypervigilance?

5

7

5

Anxiety is one of the most common problems in the world today. Haiku here about a worry you have. How often do you find yourself dwelling on it? Are you worried about something you can change, or is it something you have no power over?

5

7

5

Now write about how this nervousness feels in your body. Does your heart speed up? Do you feel jittery? Does the pace of your breathing change? Does your stomach flutter or tense up? Does your mouth get dry?

lacking warm fuzzies

we seek external comforts

breeding addiction

5

7

5

Denial, while not a feeling per se, but rather a mental process, can be a response to fear. By telling ourselves that something is not true, we permit ourselves to delete the threat from our minds. Accepting the truth can be painful (and in some cases guilt-inducing), so deciding to not perceive reality as it is can free us to live with less emotional discomfort. What's a truth you've been ignoring? Can you express it in a haiku?

tearful geisha girl

masking dislike and disgust

smiles to pleasure him

5

7

5

Interestingly, there is a relationship between fear and anger. A "mad" dog is one who is aggressive, usually because it has been beaten or abused. I believe a vicious dog is actually just a scared dog, who has lost trust that people (or other dogs) are not going to hit or attack it. I also believe that many humans who are aggressive, hateful, or vicious, have been wounded; this idea is the source of the expression "hurt people hurt people." Have you ever experienced a time when you were so anxious or afraid of something, it caused you to lash out? Write about that now.

is the cornered dog

   scared? mad? will she cower or

      bite the hand that feeds?

acknowledge the fear

   avoiding the truth hurts us

      name it to tame it

5

7

5

Prompts on Feeling Helpless

Helplessness and fear can go hand in hand. When we sense a threat but don't believe we are capable of handling it or there is no one available or willing to help us protect ourselves, we can feel disempowered. And when we feel helpless, we can feel *vulnerable.* The Latin root for this word, *vulnus,* means "wound." In the natural world, a *wounded*—physically compromised and therefore *vulnerable*—animal is more likely to be targeted than a hearty, healthy creature. Unfortunately, this is also true in the human realm; predators and bullies tend to prey upon people whom they perceive as unlikely to fight back.

we thrive having both

protection and connection

barely surviving

Trauma occurs when we feel *terrified and helpless* at the same time. If you can't escape a threat by running away, or *fleeing,* and you believe you can't confront it or *fight* it off, there is a good chance you will simply *freeze.* This "freeze response" occurs when your body becomes immobilized while simultaneously revved up with the energy that automatically and instinctively surges as part of the instinctual "fight-or-flight" response to a threat. It could be an out-of-control vehicle approaching at high speed or a bully calling you nasty names; if you don't believe that you can escape a situation and/or don't try, you might experience what we call trauma.

Trauma isn't simply a scary thing that happened; it is the fact that a terrifying event occurred, and *you were unable to stop it, escape the threat, or get immediate comfort while still in a highly aroused state.*

fighting flight and freeze

   unprotected, powerless

      fear made me fearless

child Self froze and fawned

   desperate to flee, could not fight

      vitality won

If fear doesn't dissipate, it can grow into anxiety, panic, terror, or even dread. Write a haiku about one of these intense states of fear now.

5

7

5

Prompts on Disgust

Disgust is an interesting emotion that, like fear, serves to keep us safe. Disgust is what we feel when we see, smell or taste something that could impact our health in a negative way or kill us…imagine the sight of rotting flesh or the scent of excrement. Avoiding that which causes us to experience revulsion is a fear reaction that keeps us safe, healthy and alive.

What do you find disgusting or revolting?

5

7

5

Have you ever felt disgusted by a person? We sometimes say, "so-and-so is toxic," implying that being around them is not healthy for us because our sense of comfort and safety is negatively impacted by their presence, their actions, or their words. Some people are physically revolting to us, or perhaps their language or behaviors reflect values that make us uncomfortable or contemptuous. Are there people who cause you to experience disgust or contempt?

because greed destroys

is the reason the meek shall

inherit the earth

5

7

5

Haiku is a transformative artform. By reducing complicated emotions like pain, jealousy and disgust to the simplest possible form of 17 syllables, we're able to see the more challenging parts of our Self more clearly. In allowing our pain, sorrow, and frustration to blossom into art, we take the first step toward healing by acknowledging that much of what holds us back is our own preconceptions.

Yet, as we struggle to navigate the intricate landscape of our feelings, we will inevitably encounter threads much more tangled than simple love or hate. These complicated, confusing emotions that seem to resist simple expression—these multifaceted sentiments in which joy and despair or hope and fear are blended together—present a challenge. Fortunately, haiku can serve as a bridge between the raw edges of conflicting emotions to create a truer, more wholesome understanding.

Mixed Feelings

AHH, COMPLEX EMOTIONS. It can be easier to handle emotions when they come one at a time though they may still be difficult to experience. Sadness is yucky. Anger can be unpleasant. Fear can make us feel helpless and vulnerable. I find the most challenging situations for my clients to deal with are those that cause a mixture of feelings simultaneously, *particularly feelings that are in conflict.*

the imperfect storm

    regret, grief, guilt and disgust

        I feel quite seasick

Complex emotions often result from the "cognitive disso-
nance"—defined as the state of having inconsistent thoughts,
beliefs, or attitudes—that triggers emotions. The following
haiku speaks to the fact that our lives are often not "a bed of
roses" (in fact, they are more often scary, painful, or frustrat-
ing), although many of us want to *believe* life should be easier
than it is.

amazing terror

the pain of living, the joy

of being alive

This haiku reflects my understanding of trying to live as a
"peaceful warrior."

lover *and* fighter

what to accept? to reject?

lifelong conundrum

So much of the work I do with people is comprised of acknowl-
edging and accepting that certain events which still trouble you
now in fact happened in the past, and that *it is impossible to go
back to do things over.* Wishing things had been different can
bring on a case of the "what ifs" and "if only's" which perpet-
uate rumination and frustration. Consequently, I help them

understand that, by exploring the past with an open mind and a compassionate heart, it is possible to 1) heal old wounds and 2) to make more informed and more conscious choices now and in the future that can lead to healthier outcomes for you and for your relationships.

> **rejecting what is**
>
> > **bitterness or gratitude**
> >
> > > **accepting what is**
>
> **clinging to pain is**
>
> > **"suffering of suffering"**
> >
> > > **declared the Buddha**

Are you morally committed to fidelity (*believing* that having sex with more than one person at a time is wrong) yet have considered cheating on your partner (*feeling* desire toward another)? Have you noticed that the more we love someone else (our children, a spouse, a lover), the angrier we can feel when they disappoint us or hurt us? (*Belief:* "If they really loved me too, they wouldn't do that.") Why are horror movies, which portray and even glorify fear and mayhem, beloved by so many? Can watching images of bloodshed and death make us feel more alive in some macabre fashion?

Prompts on Emotional Confusion

Can you describe how it feels to experience two conflicting emotions at the same time? Are the feelings really in conflict, or are they two sides of the same coin? Can we feel grief without having loved?

with nothing to lose

loss is so much easier

sweet, sad paradox

5

7

5

What is the difference between fear and excitement? Many people want to ride the big rollercoaster, but may be held back by some apprehension about what could happen. Will I get sick to my stomach? Will my heart pound with the extreme speed and abrupt movement? Can you write about a time where you have felt both excited and afraid?

5

7

5

A similar combination of emotions may be present at points of significant change, such as graduations. These are times when we leave behind people and routines that we've become comfortable with while approaching novelty and uncertainty. Some of us like change; some of us do not. Travelling can induce similar feelings, particularly when visiting a different culture where you don't speak the language—exciting yet nerve-wracking. Try to capture in haiku what change means for you.

5

7

5

Prompts on Unhealthy Acceptance

One of my clients, who feels anxious and on edge most of the time and wants help with stress management, described her experience by saying, "Anxiety is my friend." Although her anxiety affects her sleep, mood, energy levels, health and relationships, at times she prefers this state and dismisses the benefits of feeling calm and relaxed.

I have come to understand that this person has been conditioned to only feel "safe" when she is in high gear, taking care of the many others in her life by responding to *their* needs. We realized together that, rooted in old patterns learned in childhood as responses to traumatic events, when she senses that the people around her aren't "happy"—when they complain, or act moody, or lash out, *making her in turn feel uncomfortable, even afraid*—she anticipates their discomfort, which creates the anxious energy compelling her to fix things fast. Consequently, while she complains of feeling exhausted and overwhelmed by the many demands on her time and energy, she is simultaneously afraid to *not* prioritize others' well-being over her own.

keeping the peace with

sweetness is bittersweet when

fear of wrath drives you

Are you or someone you know a "people-pleaser" who tends to be overly-accommodating, consistently putting others' needs above their own? What might be the fear, the thought, that underlies this anxiety-related behavior?

5

7

5

Anxiety reflects the concern that something bad might happen (a fear) and I won't be able to handle it (helplessness). Does anxiety provide something beneficial for you? If you didn't experience anxiety in certain situations, what might happen? Is anxiety ever helpful, or is it (as it is for some of my clients) debilitating, causing paralysis or panic?

anxiety is

a twisting gut tornado

breathe, breathe, breathe, breathe, breathe

5

7

5

There is an inborn trait that we all possess called the negativity bias which allows us to feel prepared ("in control") for things that might happen that would in some way impact us in unanticipated and uncontrollable ways. Sadly, some of us live with high anxiety and dark anticipation too much of the time. Do you have recurring fears about what might happen?

expecting the worst

    protects from the pain of loss

        but joy is bypassed

5

7

5

Prompts on Confusion

Have you ever felt confused? Bewildered? Uncertain? As a child, were there things that just didn't make sense to you? Confusion is not knowing what to think and can lead to stagnation or paralysis—because you can't decide what to do—or dependence on another to tell you how to think and act. When I am confused, I might experience mild anxiety; to resist this, I find it beneficial to admit to and accept my confusion, creating space for the truth to surface and coalesce into something more solid and useful, enabling me to address the issue instead of feeling stuck.

    getting back to me

        assembling broken fragments

            puzzle of the soul

What confuses you? Have you ever felt perplexed by someone else's words or behaviors?

5

7

5

Confusion and uncertainty can breed anxiety. How do you experience anxiety in your body when you don't have the answers you need or control over what may happen?

5

7

5

Prompts on Guilt and Shame

Although guilt can be a useful and prosocial emotion, when misapplied, it can wreak internal havoc. Many people learn to feel guilt instead of anger, out of fear of what might happen should they respond to a situation with aggression. Being angry implies that we sense that someone else is responsible for a certain transgression and this belief *leads to a desire to take action*—speak up, stand our ground, assert ourselves, confront the doer—*in order to feel better*. Anger is arousing and can feel uncomfortable unless or until it is discharged. Yet expressing anger can escalate a situation; many folks avoid acting on their anger in order to keep themselves safe from the anger of a bigger, stronger or more powerful person. By "taking the blame," we quench the energy of our anger response. On the other hand, a few of my clients have shared that they are afraid of what they might do if they were to get in touch with their fierceness. It is possible that their feelings of guilt keep them from acting on the destructive ferocity that can erupt during self-defense.

Guilt is the emotion most humans feel when we commit an offense, or we think we have arbitrarily received more than we deserve. Guilt arises when you believe you did something wrong. Experiencing this emotion can help us become aware of a behavior that we might want to change so we don't hurt another person again. In that sense, it is a useful experience that can serve to create more positive and respectful relationships. Can you write a haiku about guilt?

I'm sorry for that

guilt weighs deep in my belly

don't do that again

5

7

5

Are you a "conflict-avoidant" person who prefers to keep the peace rather than speak up about what you perceive to be an injustice? Do you choose to blame yourself for an uncomfortable situation instead of potentially offending or upsetting the true offender? Have you ever felt guilt when, in fact, you might have been angry or offended?

5

7

5

Sometimes shame is the cause of being conflict-averse. While guilt makes you believe that you have "done something wrong," shame is the feeling that something is wrong with you. Never good enough. Not deserving. Bad. Shame is guilt magnified and powerfully internalized. When you believe that you are the guilty party in a situation, you may allow others to criticize or attack your character—while feeling defenseless—because you believe they are justified in their behavior. Try to put into words what it means for you to feel ashamed.

5

7

5

Shame can be a pervasive sense that you are guilty of wrong-doing or less-than in some way, and it can be debilitating. For example, I feel shame that—despite being a committed long-term yogi and an expert on breathing practices as well as a college-educated and environmentally-minded human who eats with attention and encourages her clients to improve self-care and wellbeing—I smoke three cigarettes a day. I know that smoking is toxic, to me, to those around me, to the environment, yet I still can't quite quit cigarettes completely. To be honest, I feel like a hypocrite. Do you ever experience shame?

5

7

5

Schadenfreude is a German word for the pleasure one gets by observing another person's misfortune, like what one might feel when a snooty, wealthy neighbor's house is vandalized. Speaking candidly, can you admit to ever feeling this way? Reflect on this. How does it feel to know you can react this way?

5

7

5

Ambivalence is feeling stuck between two thoughts, being "on the fence"—it is not simply apathy. For humans, simultaneous but contradictory thoughts, feelings or behaviors are common. Your best friend needs you to babysit her kids (caring for others), but you had a rough day at work and you really want to have a quiet night alone (self-care). You are feeling desperate to leave an abusive, long-term marriage (safety) but worried about making it on your own financially (uncertainty and fear). A man is involved with a woman who is very comfortable in her sexuality (desire) but is at the same time worried about her attraction to and for other men (jealousy). Ambivalence is at the heart of the conflict that exists in families where there are strong, contradictory political views: "I love _____ but how can they think that way?" Can you write about a time you have experienced ambivalence?

5

7

5

Untangling the knot of our more complex feelings is never easy...but framing things in haiku can often lead to new revelations. The power of brevity is the power of clarity, and a clean look at how we feel about something is essential to lasting improvement. Now, as we begin to integrate everything that we've learned, we will explore how to combine our powers of observation, expression and understatement to create new haiku that resonate with both simplicity and depth, getting to the heart of what makes us tick.

Integration:
Becoming Whole

W<small>E UNDERTOOK THIS</small> journey of self-discovery by first writing about nature and pleasant feelings before moving into more challenging emotions. Since a complete and authentic life includes taking the bitter along with the sweet, I chose to get you started with feelings that are easier to digest, then later, once you became more comfortable writing in the haiku format, introduced emotions that can be harder to bite into and chew on.

> **on the conscious path**
>
> **roots and rocks are my teachers**
>
> **dig deep, climb over**

Since wholeness includes exploring and accepting *all* parts of our Selves, not just the desirable or the comfortable, I wanted to prepare you to examine the aspects that you may struggle to acknowledge. Such parts might be responsible for what is called *self-aversion.* If we look deeply enough, we all have thoughts and feelings that "ain't so pretty," yet I believe that *it is impossible to be whole if we ignore or dismiss the parts of ourselves that we may not like or actually reject.*

Integration requires self-knowledge and self-acceptance, and is the opposite of fragmentation. If we choose to ignore or reject the parts of ourselves that we don't like, we cannot feel complete. Self-discovery via writing is a pathway to authentic living.

> **when I'm me with you**
>
> **and you are you with me too**
>
> **authenticity**

> **no mud, no lotus**
>
> **no storm, no rainbow…the dark**
>
> **can nourish beauty**

Now, let's take what you have done and pull back to gain some perspective on what makes you you. What have you learned about your Self in this process of exploring your emotional depths? Can you craft a few haikus about the self-knowledge you have acquired?

5

7

5

5

7

5

Prompts About My Self

What emotions challenge you? Which feelings do you experience with frequency? Which emotions were hard to explore, maybe bringing you to tears or creating anxiety? Were any of these topics too arousing or intense for you, causing you to feel overwhelmed?

5

7

5

5

7

5

5

7

5

This is where our true work begins. In yoga, it is said that the poses you least enjoy doing are the ones you most need to open up and become stronger and more flexible. The same goes for "emotional yoga." Did you feel on the brink of "losing control" or "freaking out" as you pondered your truths? ("I never knew that I…") What did you enjoy writing about?

deep diving inward

found a treasure chest, full of

gold and rust and love

5

7

5

5

7

5

Authenticity and Challenge

Over the course of these exercises, were you able to "talk" about things that you had never "verbalized" before? Did you think about things you hadn't thought about in a long time? Grief and sadness are particularly difficult for many of us to experience. If you grew up in or currently exist in environments where being vulnerable or soft or tender makes you a target for other people's attention—be it positive, like compassion, or negative, like aggression or judgment—you might feel ill at ease about sharing your pain. "So you're *sad*? Well I'll give you something to cry about!" taunted a dismissive parent.

When a well-meaning someone, trying to comfort us, suggests, "Don't be sad, it's okay," or, "It could be worse, count your blessings," hearing such attempts might only make us feel worse about what we are experiencing, as if our hurt is unnecessary or excessive. Often a reflection of unease with their own sensitivity or sense of helplessness, such remarks belie the other person's discomfort with our distress and their reluctance to be present with someone else's pain.

paying attention

 to war, hatred, cruelty

  is painful…breathe peace

Sometimes the best we can do is make space for another's (and our own) suffering. My best friend has muscular sclerosis, and it is lately progressing quickly. In her late fifties and living alone, she is trying to balance the reality of her rapidly declining health with the contentment and hope she would prefer to experience despite facing a loss of independence, constant fatigue, and the grief of her "golden years" being tarnished. I wrote this haiku for her:

we laugh about life

and we laugh about death too

ha ha ha ha ha!

Numerous clients of mine have confided that they do not like to ask for help when they are struggling, typically because "I don't want to be a burden," *especially when their friends or family members are struggling too.* When possible, however, I believe that we can decide to "suffer together." Although we can't fix every problem we confront, *we can* support one another through the difficulties that Life presents. Etymologically, the word *compassion* means "to suffer with."

is your relief my

burden? no, the open heart

can catch and release

not hope but solace

sharing deep enduring pain

commiseration

Have you noticed a tendency to keep your troubles to yourself? Do you struggle to share your emotions with others? Are there only a few people you are comfortable opening up to? Only one person? No one?

5

7

5

Of course, sometimes when we try to talk about our sadness in an attempt to defuse its charge, the listener minimizes our pain by implying that they have it worse; this behavior is called "one-downmanship." This response can stop us in our emotional tracks and teach us to *not* reach out and share our concerns with others for fear that they, stuck in their own negativity, aren't listening, don't care, will diminish our need, or will reject our pain.

Why do we sometimes invalidate others' feelings? Perhaps because, if we are uncomfortable acknowledging tenderness in ourselves, we tend to downplay or bypass our own need for comfort or understanding. When someone complains about an issue and we counter with "Oh, you think that's bad? Well I…," this response is one-downmanship, an indirect way to share your pain *when you are not able to be direct about and clearly state what it is that you need.* (A hug? a kind word? company? comfort? simply to be heard?)

The truth is, we all suffer at one time or another; is it possible to simply be compassionate and listen with an open heart to one another as needed?

spirit speaks through acts

    compassion, respect, love, from

        heart to heart to heart

I have learned over the years that the surest way to learn to be compassionate with *others* is by first developing compassion *for our own Selves:* acceptance without judgment of all of our emotional states, the negative as well as the positive. That is why I created this workbook. Only through self-exploration, self-understanding and, ultimately, self-acceptance, can we accept others in *all* of their ways of being.

    integrated Self

        radical acceptance of

           each and every part

One goal of this workbook is to help you think about and write about your emotions in order to *become more comfortable with the discomfort* that might arise. In therapy, a common goal is to build "distress tolerance" so that we can slowly permit ourselves to experience the emotions we typically do not want to feel.

Instead of reacting unconsciously to a "trigger" and responding automatically (yelling at or attacking another, walking or running away, reaching for a drink, or distracting ourselves), discovering and acknowledging what our personal triggers are enables us to 1) avoid them in the first place, 2) anticipate a strong reaction in order to plan for a healthy response to that reaction, or 3) learn to ride the wave of the surfacing emotion *without our intense feelings controlling us.*

hiding self from self

what you don't know CAN hurt you

hold your fears with love

After completing these exercises, have you noted a tendency to distract yourself as uncomfortable ideas arise? To suppress thoughts or emotions? Did you uncover any repressed material as you unpacked feelings and memories? Repression happens subconsciously and automatically while suppression is more of a conscious choice: "I don't like feeling _____, so I'll leave/smoke a joint/sleep/hang up/ watch a movie, etc." Did you find yourself wanting to avoid certain topics or emotions? Did a particular person, event, memory, or situation come up with frequency in the course of writing? If so, haiku about that here.

resisting what is

instead of surrendering

makes your heels bloody

distract myself? nope

paying attention demands

focused awareness

5

7

5

Were there certain periods in your life where a particular emotion was experienced more than others? As we get older, we may become more resilient to things that used to upset us, having learned to "pick our battles" or "not sweat the little things." Meanwhile, there may be situations or people that continue to elicit strong negative reactions in us throughout our lives.

Some folks might find that they lose the capacity to feel deeply, either by choice or through ennui. A few of my middle-aged clients have lamented that they have lost the ability to feel awe or bliss. Whether it is a learned response to soften the pain of disappointment or the result of "having seen it all" (though I think they are just not looking), my hope is that each and every one of us can feel deeply and broadly until we expire.

openness to awe

> **the awful and the awesome**

>> **the guts and glories**

apathy works by

> **quenching the heat of pain yet**

>> **joyous light eclipsed**

acceptance and awe

> **taking the bad with the good**

>> **the path of wisdom**

Just For Fun

IN THIS SECTION, I offer a few expressions or concepts that may inspire you to write some haikus. No guidance necessary; you're on your own here. Below, you will find lists of five and seven syllable words and expressions that might whet your creative appetite.

Five-Syllable Words

These are perfect to start or end a haiku:

negativity	spontaneity	imagination
commiseration	dehumanizing	positivity
authenticity	generosity	hypocritical
opportunity	humiliation	reciprocity
kaleidoscopic	personality	unbelievable!
curiosity	hallucination	creativity
emancipation	animosity	sensitivity

5

7

5

5

7

5

Five-Syllable Expressions

The following are some "jumping-off points" to either start or end off a haiku:

"it takes a village"

"there's no place
    like home"

"no one's laughing now"

"it is what it is"

"when life gets you down"

"practice what you preach"

"the moment of truth"

"the show must go on"

"ignorance is bliss"

"a word to the wise"

"I am what I am"

"only time will tell"

"old habits die hard"

"I'm shit out of luck"

"enough is enough"

"take it or leave it"

"I learned the hard way"

5

7

5

5

7

5

Seven-Syllable Words and Expressions

Of course, with seven syllables, these words and expressions can become the middle line of a haiku. You can also break the phrases up, if you prefer.

super sensitivity

artificiality

individuality

inevitability

irresponsibility

"sticks and stones may
   break my bones"

"to be perfectly honest"

"peace, love and
   understanding"

"all that glitters is
   not gold"

"the only way out
   is through"

"ignorance can be blissful"

"what you don't know can't
   (or can) hurt you"

"do what it takes
   to survive"

"be careful what you
   wish for"

"let's agree to disagree"

"that was then and
   this is now"

"blood is thicker than water"

"I took the road less travelled"

"it's not as hard as you think"

"can't (or can!) teach an old dog new tricks"

5

7

5

5

7

5

5

7

5

Haiku Activities for Daily Life

If you enjoyed the work you have done here, or at least benefitted from thinking and writing about your emotions in this way, and want to continue to explore within, you may consider doing one of the following:

Write a daily haiku. Whether in the morning to inspire yourself to have a good day or at bedtime to process the day's events, writing a single haiku each day can do wonders to bring the day's events into focus and help you reflect on (or plan for) the gifts of the day.

Glimmer vs trigger. To practice acknowledging then letting go of the negative in order to invite in and make space for the positive, you might try writing one cheerful haiku expressing happiness, joy, or calmness and one negative poem to externalize your sad, scared, or angry thoughts and emotions *every day*.

Destruction and creation. What would make your life better *if you could let go of it*? What do you need more of to feel balanced, relaxed and peaceful? This is simply an exercise in heartstorming, letting the "if only's" have a voice. There is no need to follow through on your ideas; however, making space to visualize and ponder a different, better, future can be the seed for change and transformation.

> fault lines shear through roots
>
> patterns set in stone crumble
>
> earthquake of the Self

Write a haiku about something you are proud of about yourself. What do you excel at? What makes you think "Damn I'm good?" This may not necessarily be something that other folks appreciate; however, the truth of your own Self is what matters here, and always.

Write a haiku about a character strength you possess. This could be patience, humility, perseverance, compassion, loyalty, etc. If none of these inspire you, try writing about one you would like to develop.

Compose your own mantra to guide you during your day. Use self-affirming language if you struggle with self-doubt; choose calming words if you feel stressed a lot or struggle to fall or stay asleep. By designing your own mantras, you can tailor them to your particular needs and bring them to mind as necessary.

> breathe in slow and deep
>
> expand open fill with light
>
> breathe out melt melt melt

Be funny. We can write haikus that are humorous or intended to amuse, perhaps taking inspiration from limericks.

Lo-kus. A friend and I were once exchanging haikus that ended up focusing on sex as subject matter. At the time, I joked that they should be called "low-kus," which made us laugh, too! My point is—in contrast to the high art of writing classic or traditional haikus—it's okay to use the 5-7-5 syllable format to write about anything you want! A rubber ball, the taste of cinnamon, a funny-looking cloud...spontaneous expression via what I call "poetic licentiousness!"

> **are my hot flashes**
>
> > **"endogenous pyrogens"**
> >
> > > **unrequited lust?**

> **spirit rising**
>
> > **through resurrected libido**
> >
> > **your touch is divine**

Use song lyrics. Incorporate ones that hit you hard or inspire you. Although Joni Mitchell's 1969 classic "Woodstock" was written about learning to live peacefully, this haiku is about my bitterness that humanity seems to not have realized the dream of world peace and harmony...yet.

> **"back to the garden"?**
>
> > **we never left but instead**
> >
> > > **s*** in our own bed**

Final Thoughts

THE GREATEST GIFT for me as a psychotherapist is hearing a client say, "I think I'm okay now." Whether we've worked together for a month or for years, it is a heartfelt and soul-deep thrill to know that the empathetic and non-judgmental space that I provide has truly helped this person start to heal. Creating a safe haven for people to dig deep into their fears, to experience vulnerability, to learn how to face their wounds and their scabs with self-compassion—and to imagine that their life could be better—is deeply satisfying. It makes my heart sing to assist them in accessing the courage to live with radical acceptance and to make the necessary changes to feel more balanced and alive.

I know how it feels to be stuck, to experience helplessness, and to be afraid. Through expressive writing we can, at least to some degree, be our own therapist…as long as we remain open-hearted (empathetic) and open-minded (non-judgmental) toward our Selves while daring to share our truths and bare our souls on paper.

Has your process of self-discovery been challenging? Did self-expression flow like a river or feel dammed up? Did your "you" become clearer as you peeled away layers of self-ignorance? Were you able to excavate parts of yourself you did not realize existed inside, thoughts and feelings that were submerged and foreign but are now surfaced and friendly? By shining a light on previously "dark" material, I hope you have improved your ability to tolerate distress with equanimity by surfing the waves of changing emotion. Remember: the meaning of "to heal" is "to make whole." Do you feel more whole, more complete, more integrated than when you began this deep dive into Self?

focused expansion

balance constantly shifting

flexible nature

It is my hope that Healing With Haiku has been a helpful part of your path toward self-knowledge and inner peace. There exist innumerable ways to address and strengthen our emotional functioning: yoga, breathwork, meditation, a faith practice, therapy, grounding in nature, movement and exercise, addressing sleep challenges, caring for a pet, any sort of artistic expression, to name just a few!

Of course, many of us find that writing is therapeutic. While a lot of people I know journal, I find that writing haiku is a more effective way to express myself. Due to its concise nature, I have to really check in with my thoughts and feelings in order to focus in on what I need to communicate. Crafting haiku functions like a mini-meditation, one that assists me in sharing a concept in just three short lines. I write and rewrite until this 17 syllable non-rhyming poem makes sense…at least to me. Because ultimately, although I have shared many of my own haikus in this book, I wrote each and every one because I was struggling or inspired or moved. It was never my intention to publish, but the teacher/helper/artist in me converged to offer this workbook to you, because haiku has helped—and continues to help—me to heal. May it help you, too!

About the Author

Anne Helfer is a 60-something mother, wife, artist, teacher, yogi and healer. She has worked with children and adults as a social worker and mental health therapist, always with the goal of empowering everyone to live more authentically. By helping each individual discover who they truly are in order to develop their unique strengths while acknowledging and addressing their personal challenges, she has witnessed transformations—large and small—in how her clients relate to themselves, to the people in their lives and to the world around them. Self-compassion and dignity for all are her guideposts. As the author of *Eat Well, Sleep Better, Move More: A Journey of Self-Care*, Anne strives to live by what she calls "The Silver Rule": "*Do unto yourself as you would do unto others.*"

haiku practice

5

7

5

5

7

5

5

7

5

5

7

5

haiku practice

5

7

5

5

7

5

5

7

5

5

7

5

haiku practice

5

7

5

5

7

5

5

7

5

5

7

5

haiku practice

5

7

5

5

7

5

5

7

5

5

7

5

haiku practice

5

7

5

5

7

5

5

7

5

5

7

5

haiku practice

5

7

5

5

7

5

5

7

5

5

7

5

haiku practice

5

7

5

5

7

5

5

7

5

5

7

5